MONEY ISN'T EVERYTHING

Unless You Can't Find Your Credit Card

by

T. Alexander Anderson

TMPress, Inc.

COPYRIGHT © 2004 by TMPress, Inc.
All rights reserved. No part of this book may be used or reproduced
or transmitted in any form or by any means, electronic or mechanical, including
photocopying, recording, or by any information storage and
retrieval system, without written permission from the publisher.

Published by TMPress, Inc., 9256 Black Oaks Court, Maple Grove, MN 55311

TMPress books may be purchased for educational, business, or sales promotional use.
For information write TMPress, Inc., Marketing Department,
9256 Black Oaks Court, Maple Grove, MN 55311
e-mail: themoneybooks@hotmail.com
Printed by Ideal Printers, Inc., St. Paul, MN, U.S.A.

Library of Congress Cataloging-in-Publication data
Anderson, T. Alexander
Money isn't everything : unless you can't find
your credit card / by T. Alexander Anderson — 1st ed.
p. cm. - (The Money Books ; 1)
LCCN 2003097004
ISBN 0-9706856-1-0
1. Finance, Personal-United States-Humor
2. Quality of life-United States-Humor. I. Title.
HG179.A55985 2004   332.024'0207
QB103-200812
10 9 8 7 6 5 4 3 2 1

PREFACE

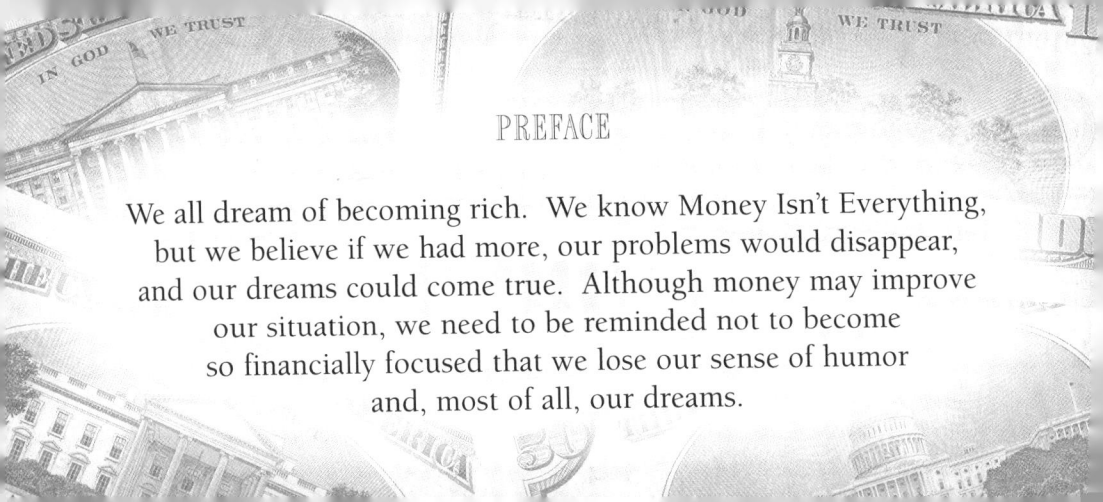

We all dream of becoming rich. We know Money Isn't Everything, but we believe if we had more, our problems would disappear, and our dreams could come true. Although money may improve our situation, we need to be reminded not to become so financially focused that we lose our sense of humor and, most of all, our dreams.

Money Isn't Everything not only gives us building blocks for wealth, it reminds us not to take money to seriously. The companion books to *Money Isn't Everything*, *Money Doesn't Buy Happiness* and *It's Only Money*, provide more of the necessary building blocks for wealth. These books could be the best money you ever spend.

May all your dreams come true,

T. Alexander Anderson

FOR SHAWN

If we want a fatter wallet,
we need to remove our credit cards.

Easy payments are never cheap.

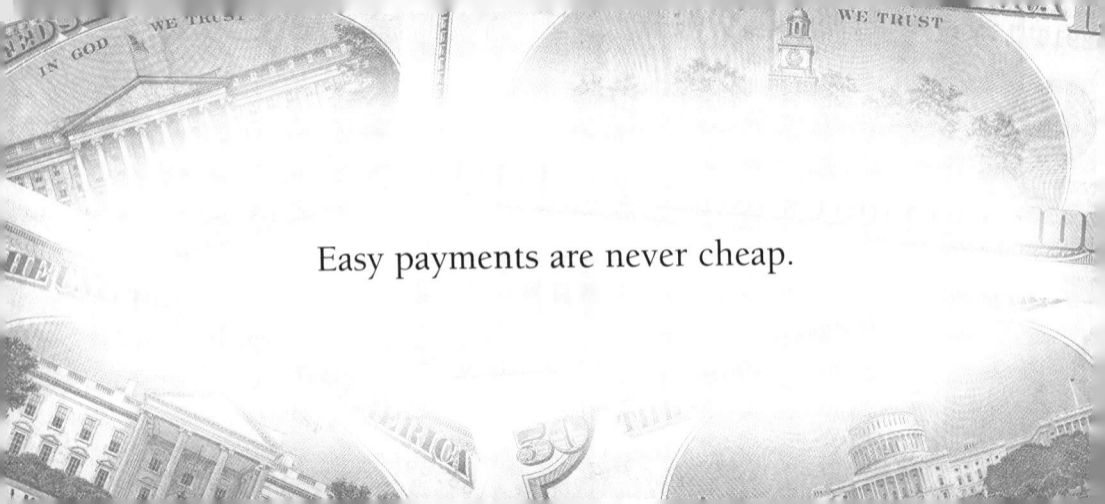

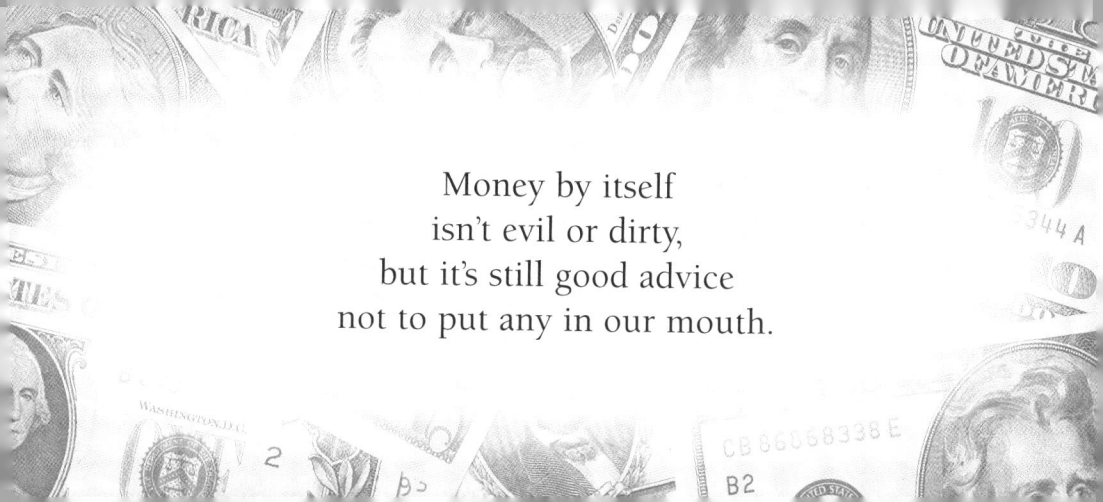

Money by itself
isn't evil or dirty,
but it's still good advice
not to put any in our mouth.

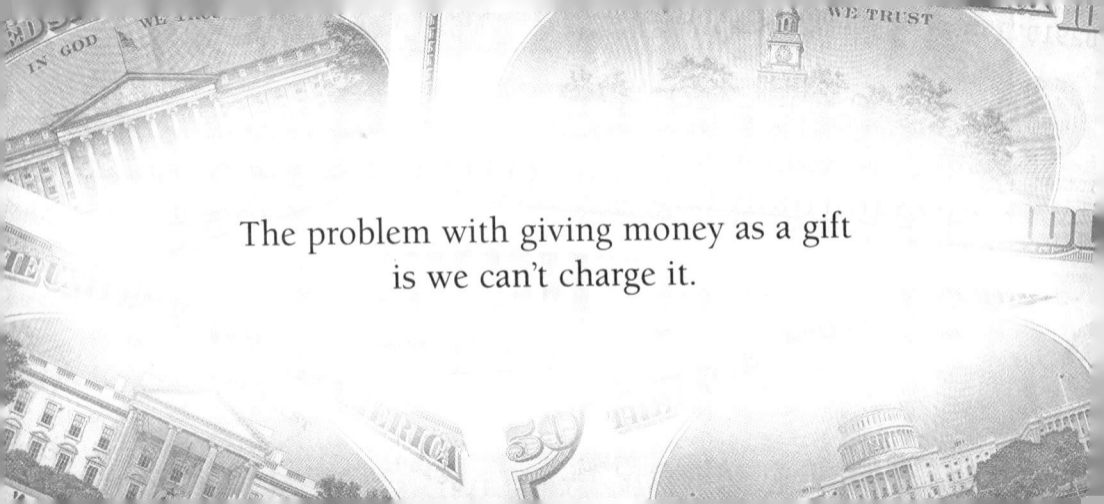

The problem with giving money as a gift is we can't charge it.

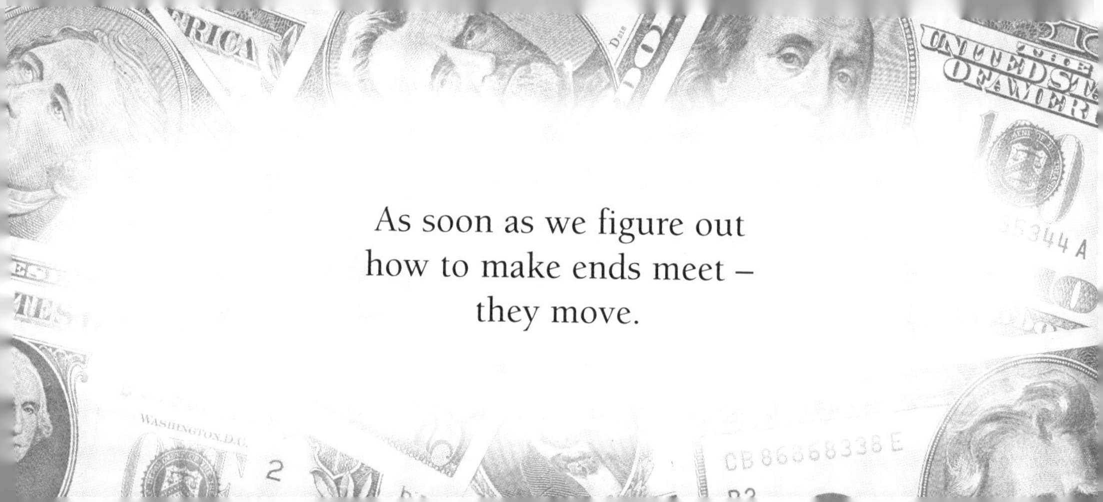

As soon as we figure out
how to make ends meet –
they move.

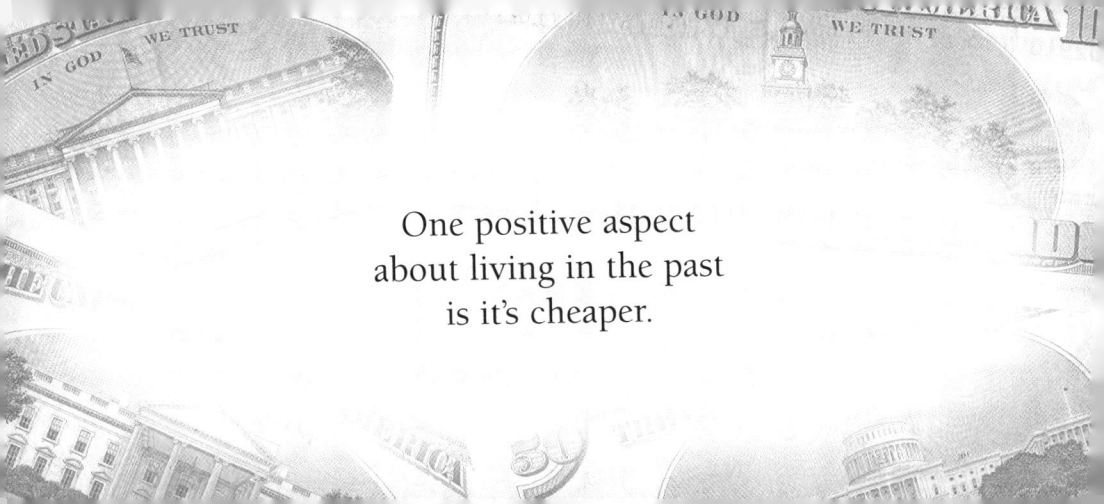

One positive aspect
about living in the past
is it's cheaper.

A dollar can go a long way,
especially, if we lend it to someone.

Ignorance is more expensive than education.

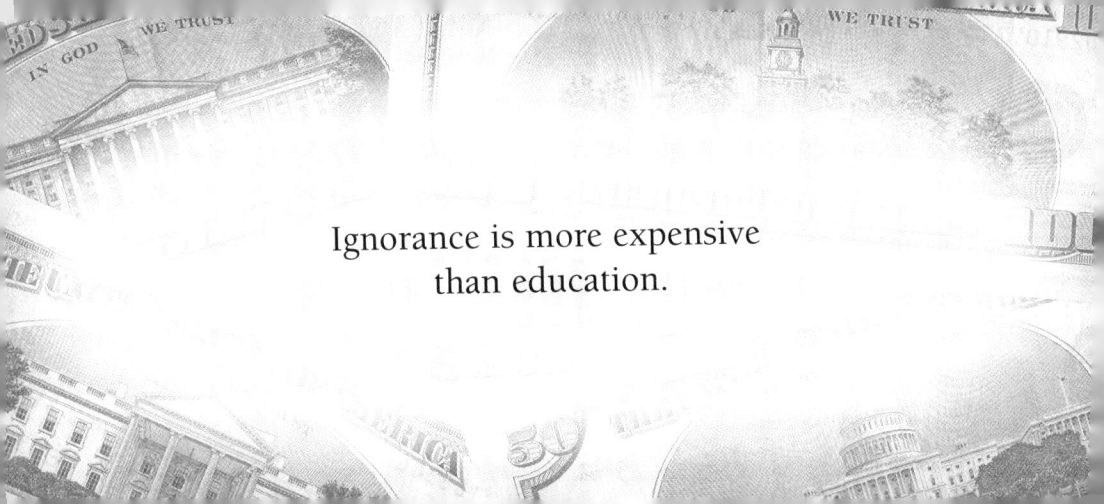

A warranty is something we need to buy that we will never need because we know if we don't buy it, we will need it.

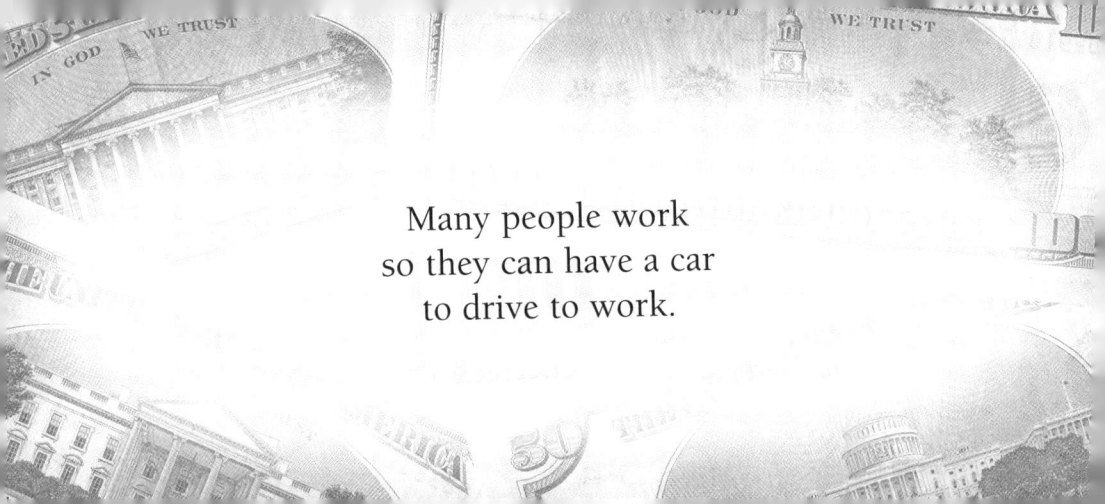

Many people work
so they can have a car
to drive to work.

The best way to negotiate
is to let the other side speak first.

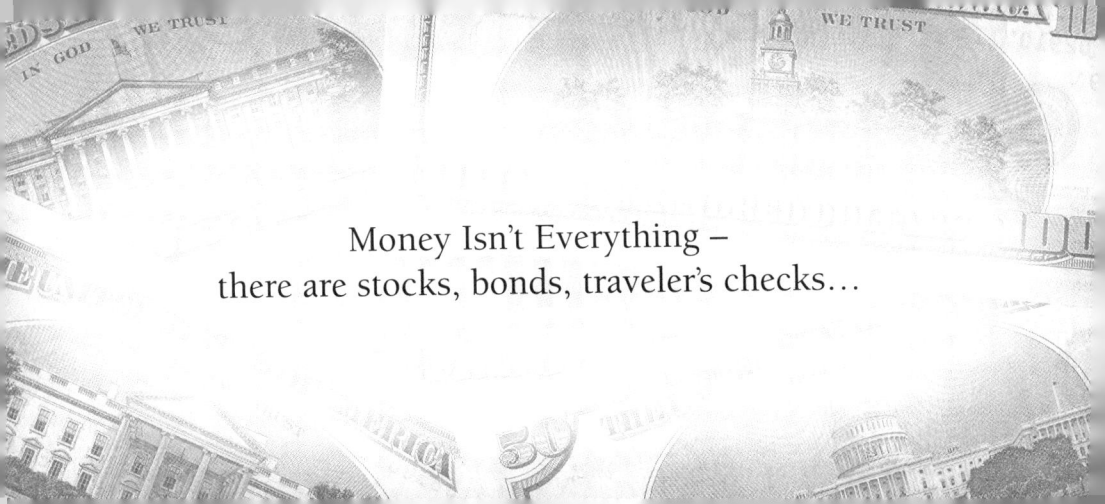

Money Isn't Everything –
there are stocks, bonds, traveler's checks…

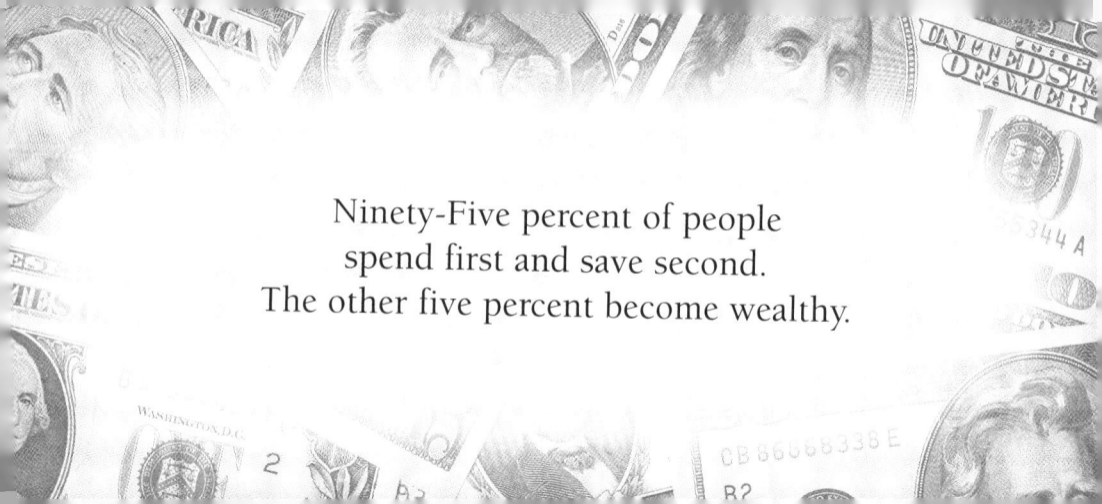

Ninety-Five percent of people
spend first and save second.
The other five percent become wealthy.

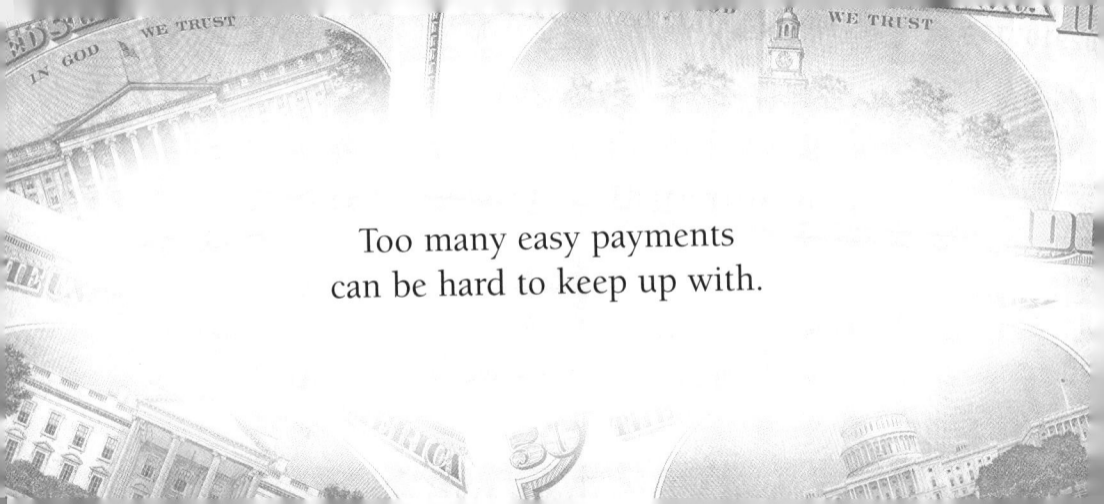

Too many easy payments
can be hard to keep up with.

Inflation is when we put off till tomorrow what we could do today, and when tomorrow comes we can't afford it.

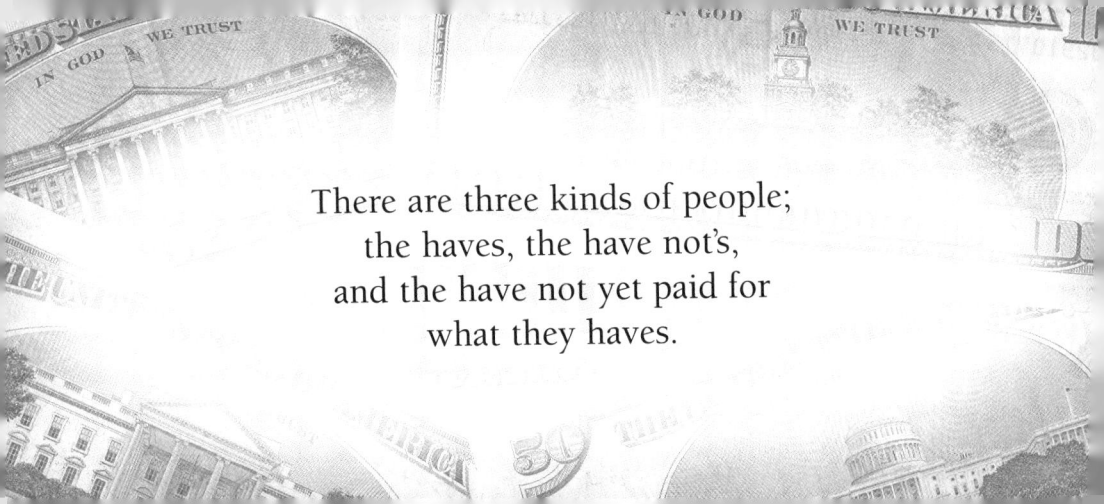

There are three kinds of people;
the haves, the have not's,
and the have not yet paid for
what they haves.

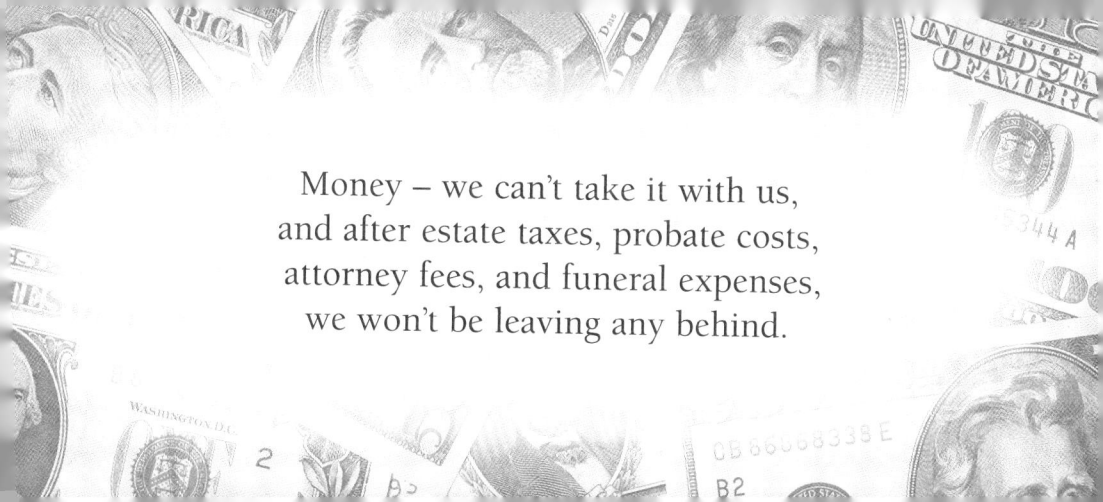

Money – we can't take it with us,
and after estate taxes, probate costs,
attorney fees, and funeral expenses,
we won't be leaving any behind.

Remember when the cost of living was only everything we made?

Money can cover
a lot of defects
in a person.

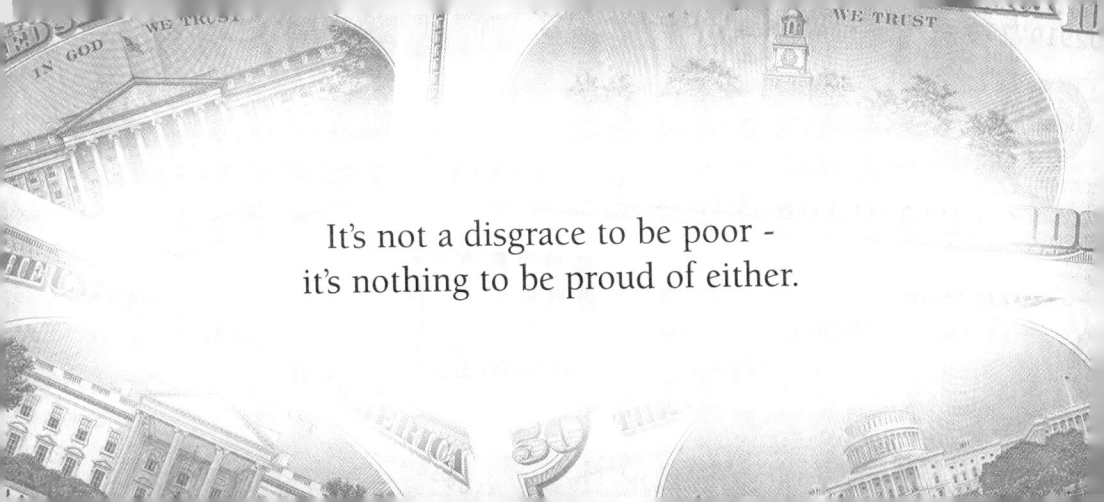

It's not a disgrace to be poor -
it's nothing to be proud of either.

Money is the stuff dreams are made of.

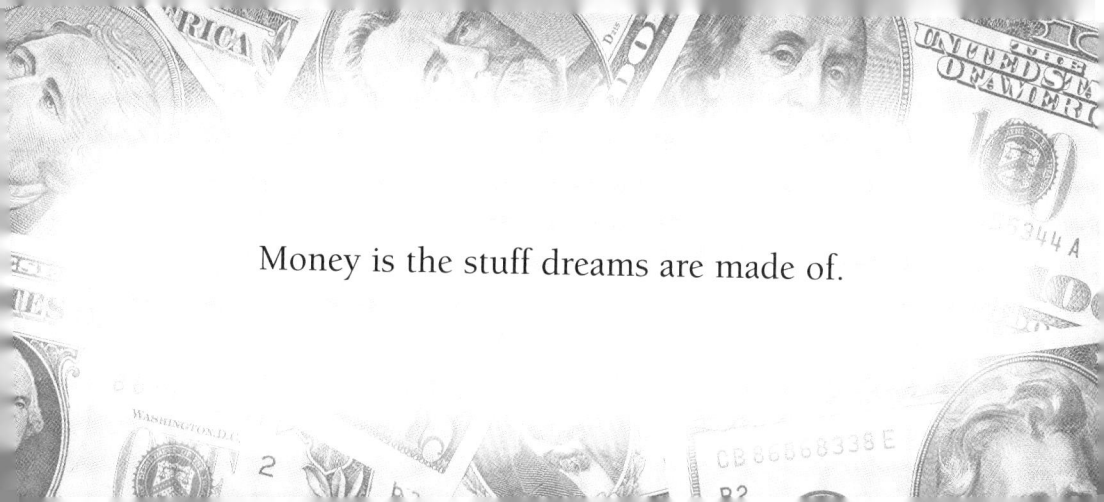

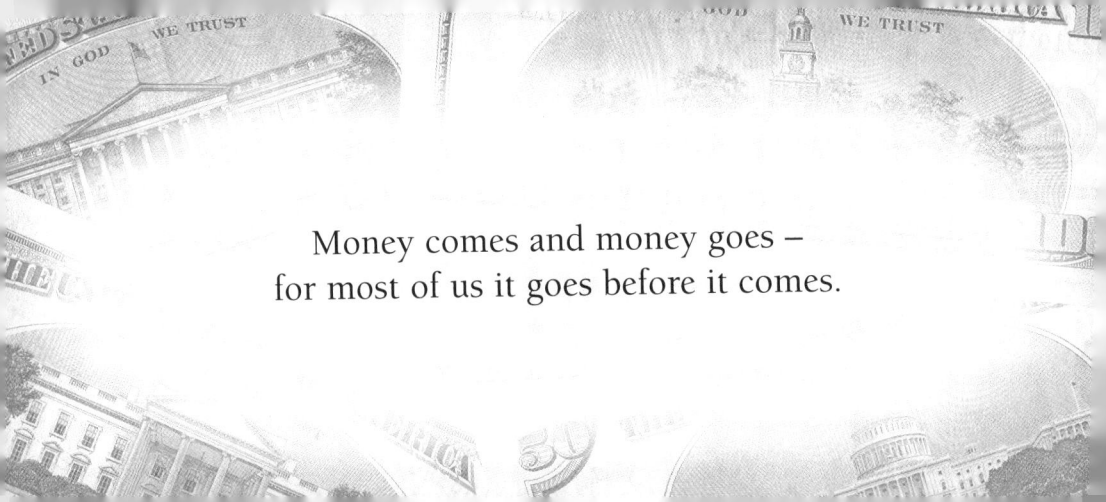

Money comes and money goes —
for most of us it goes before it comes.

If we do what we love,
the money will follow.
We just can't rely on it as
our only source of income.

Credit cards allow us to pretend
we are not broke.

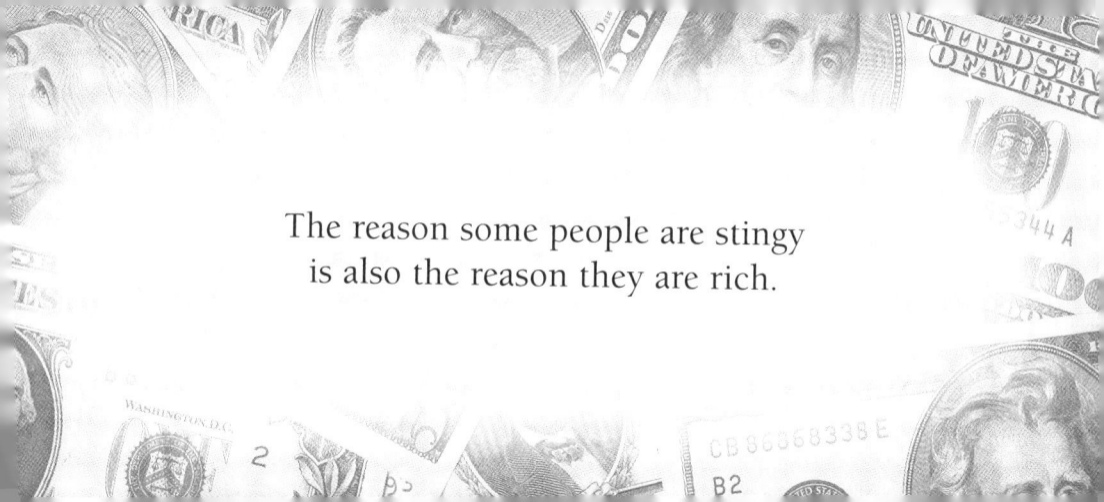

The reason some people are stingy
is also the reason they are rich.

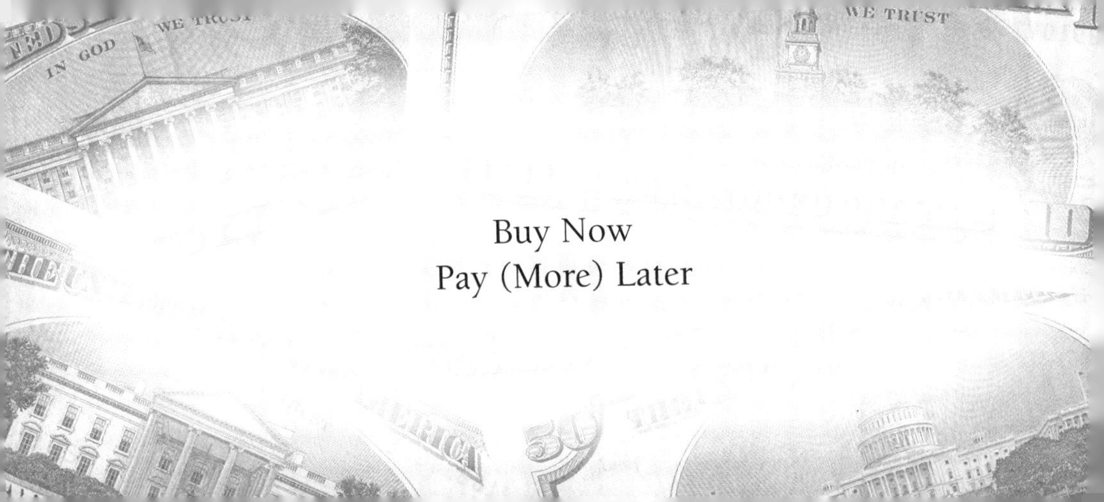

Buy Now
Pay (More) Later

If money grew on trees,
they would be in someone else's yard.

Possessions can possess us.

Investing money is so complex
even financial advisors
need financial advisors.

Money Isn't Everything,
but it's getting more difficult
to do everything without it.

Spending more than we make
is like driving down the wrong way
on a one way dead end street.

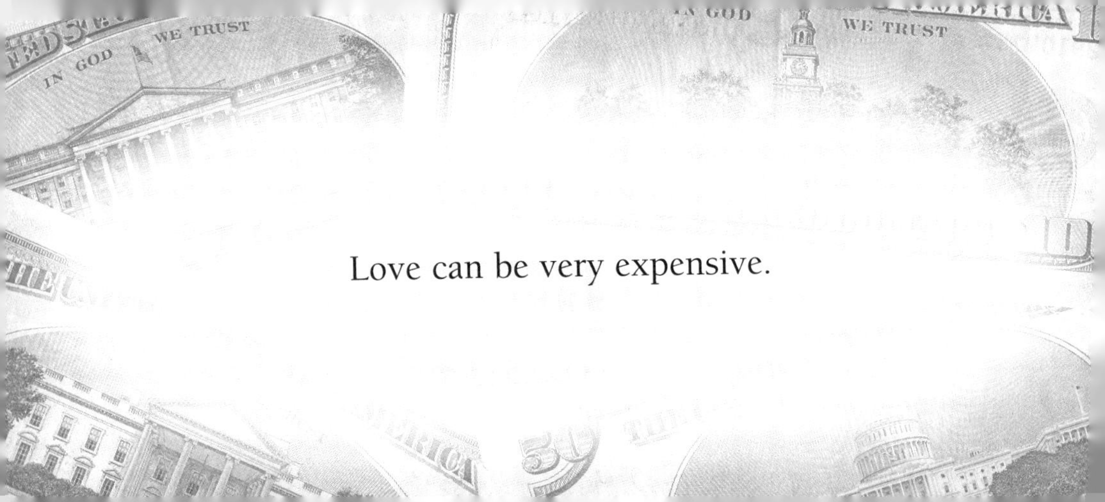

Love can be very expensive.

Most of us are at the airport
when our ship comes in.

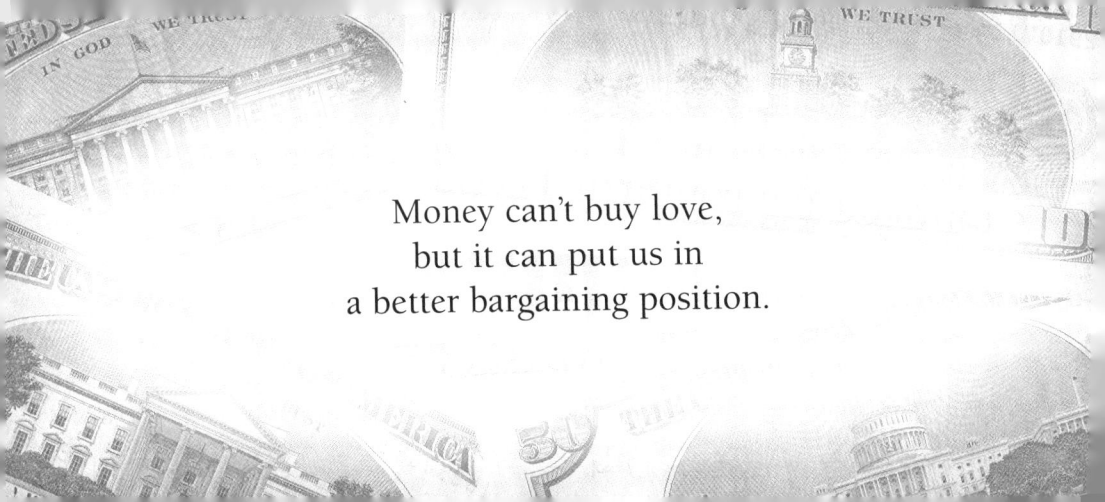

Money can't buy love,
but it can put us in
a better bargaining position.

If we gotta have it now –
we won't have much later.

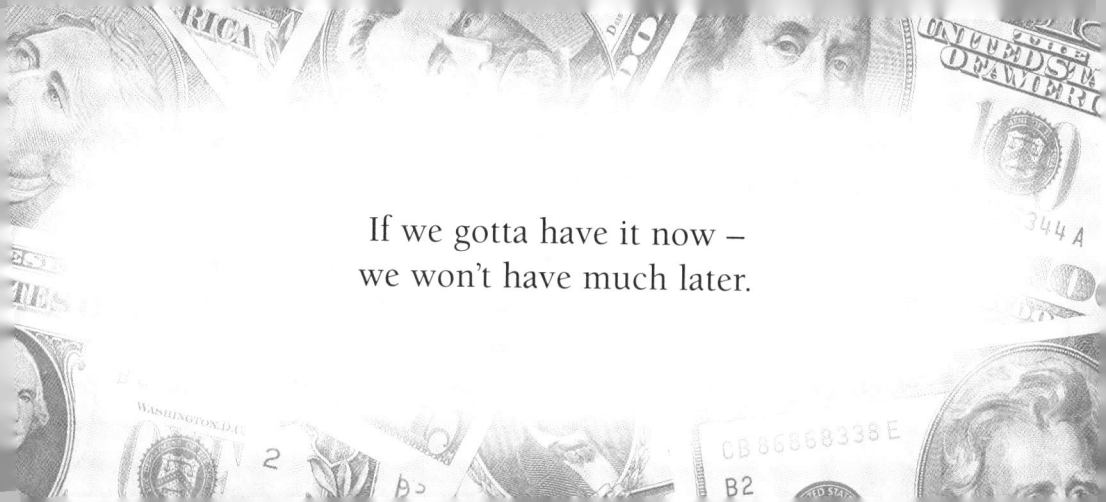

Those who think money can do anything
will probably do anything for money.

The best deals are often
the ones we didn't make.

If we keep buying what we don't need,
we'll end up needing what we
can no longer afford to buy.

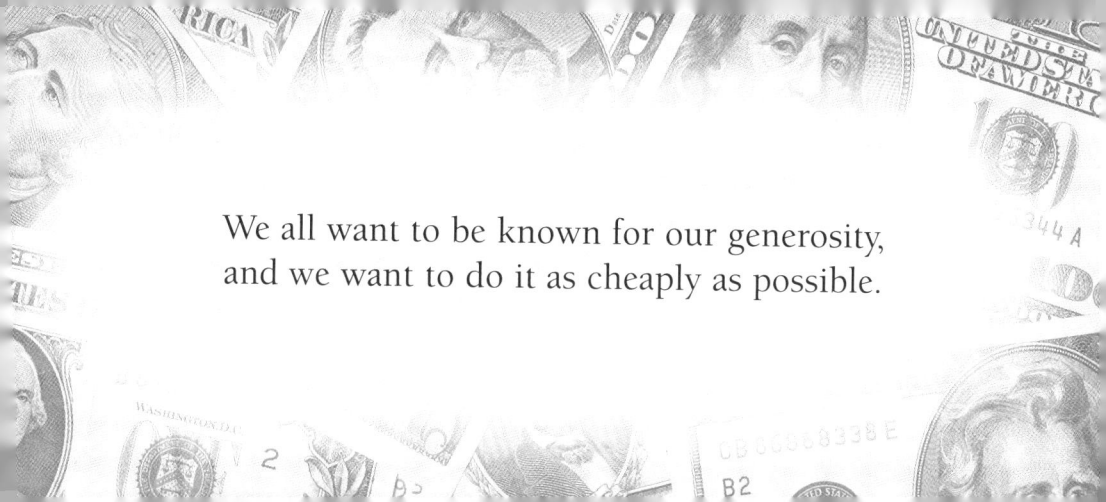

We all want to be known for our generosity,
and we want to do it as cheaply as possible.

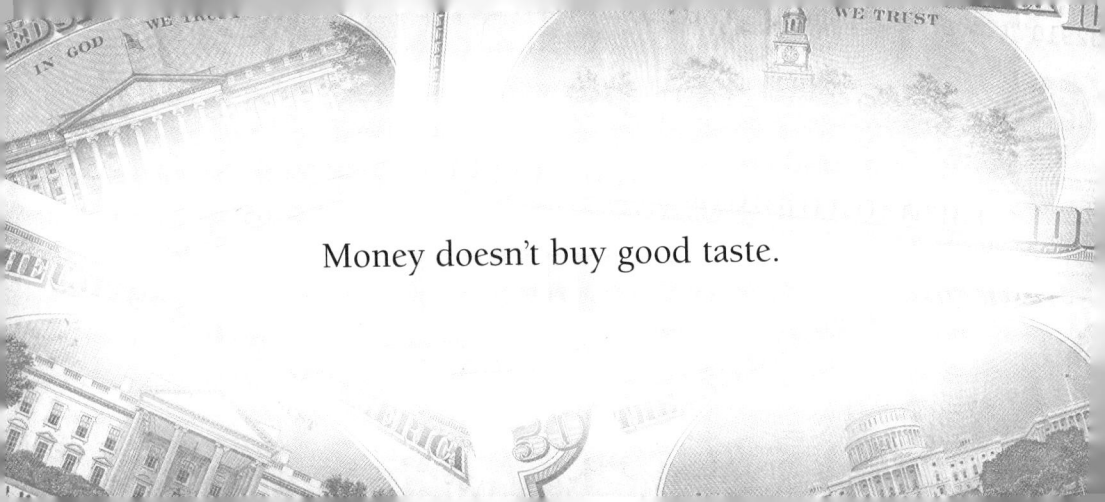

Money doesn't buy good taste.

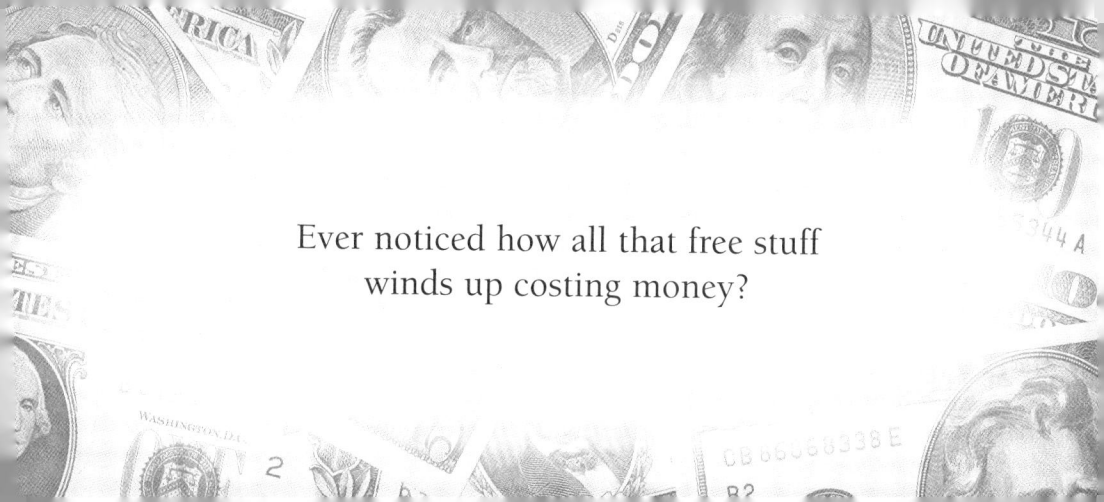

Ever noticed how all that free stuff winds up costing money?

The only thing more annoying
than a poor loser
is a rich winner.

We must learn from the investing mistakes of others because we won't have enough money to make them all on our own.

A lot of people want to become filthy rich,
but few get the second part.

Life is like eating a liver sandwich.
If we have enough bread,
we won't taste the liver.

Poverty is genetic.
We get it from our children.

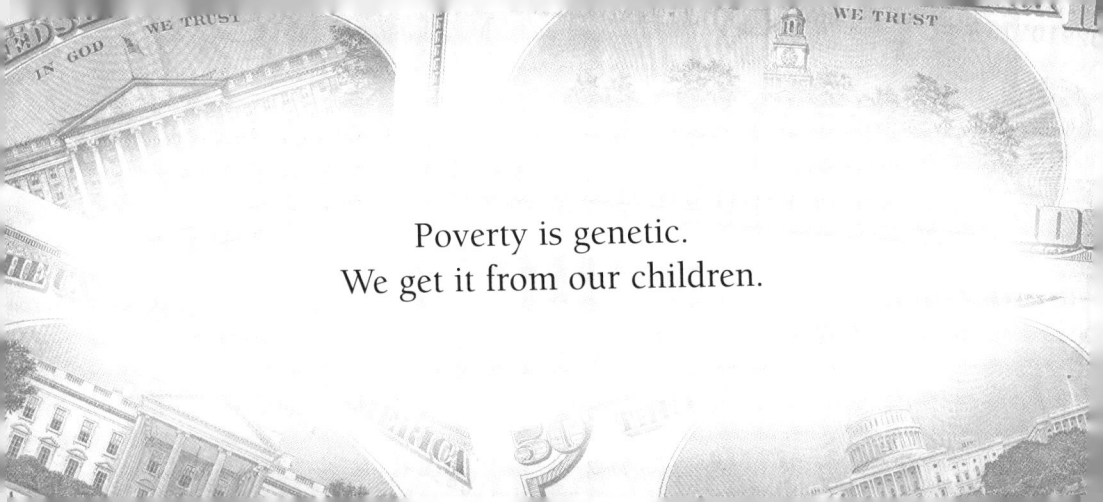

The rich are rich because
the poor are poor.

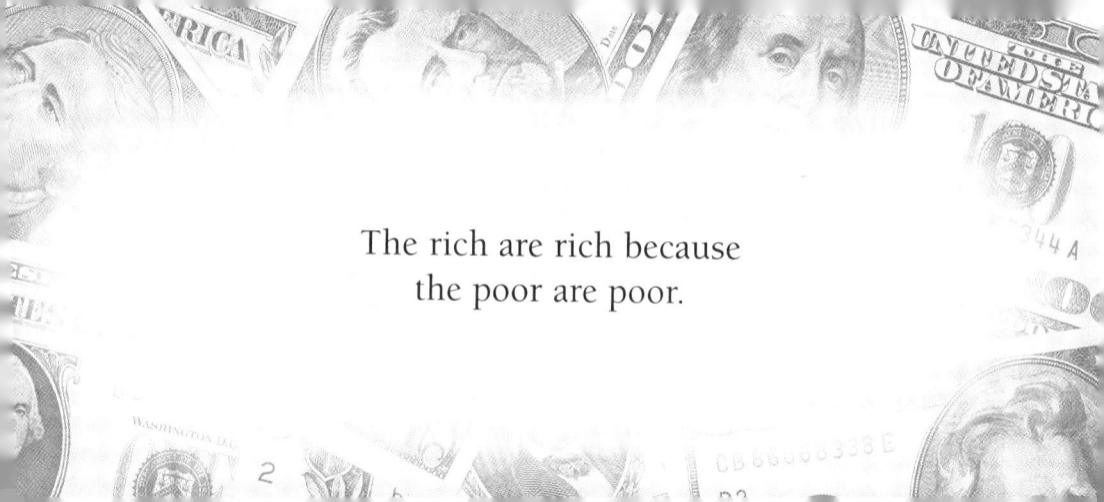

Those who marry for money –
Earn It.

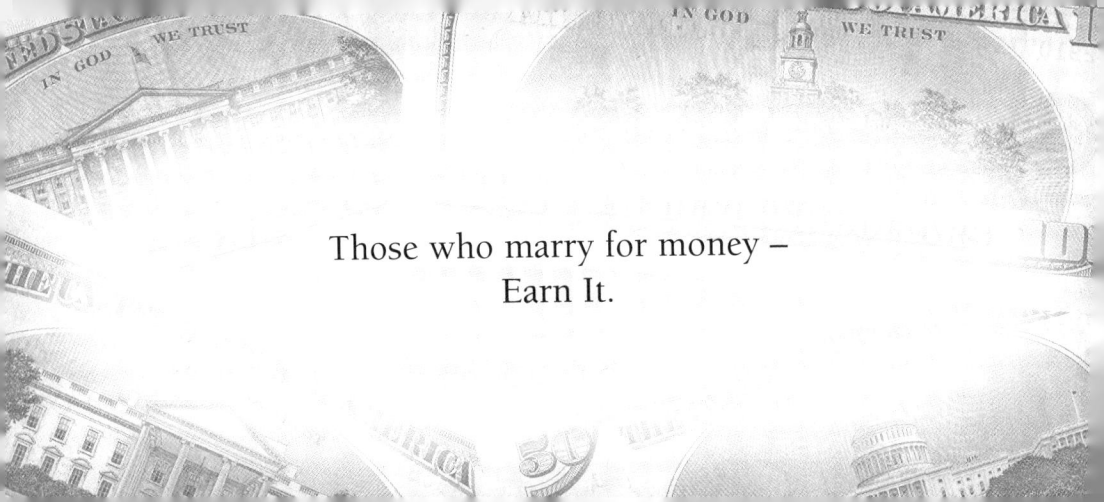

It's easy to sit around and dream
what we would like to do
if we had a lot of money,
but it won't make us rich.

There is always free cheese in a mousetrap, but it's the second mouse that gets it.

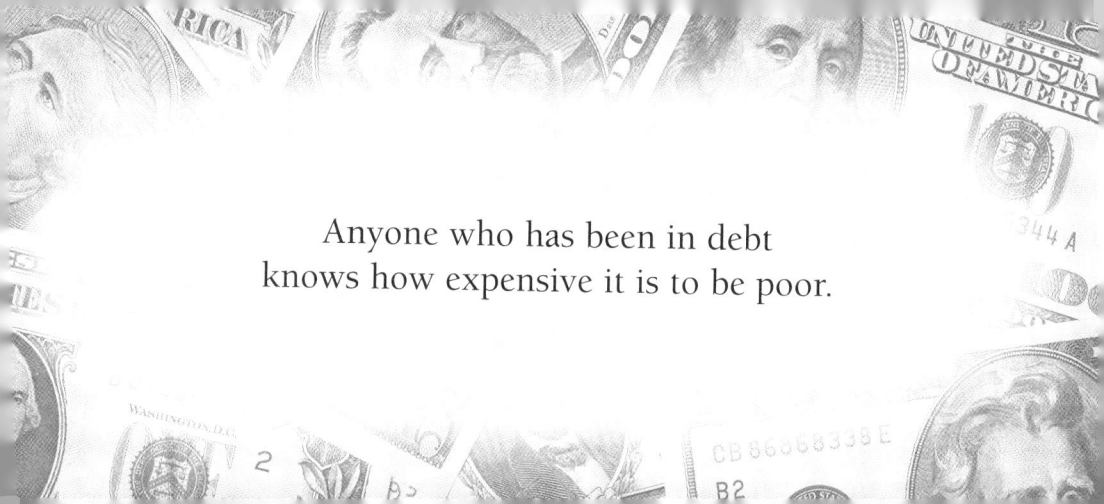

Anyone who has been in debt
knows how expensive it is to be poor.

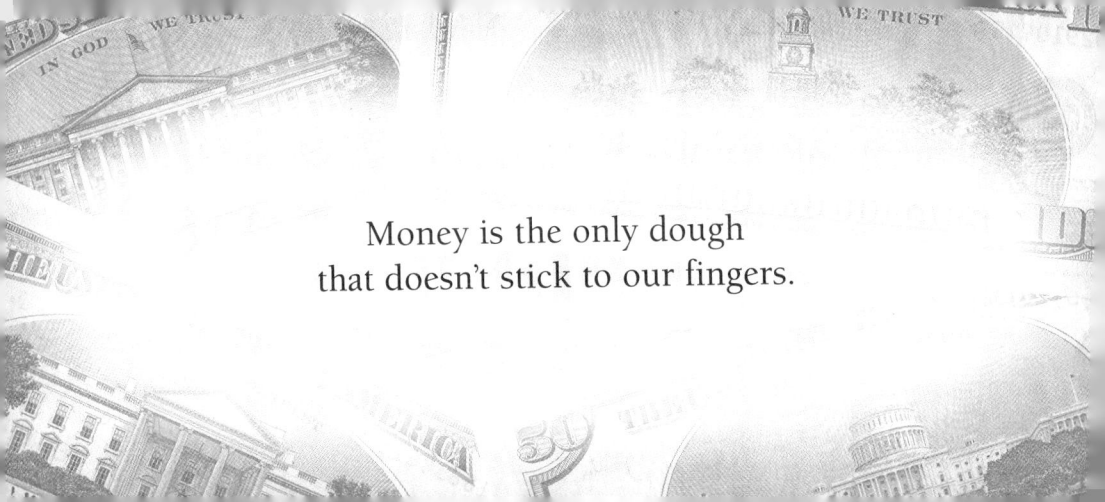

Money is the only dough
that doesn't stick to our fingers.

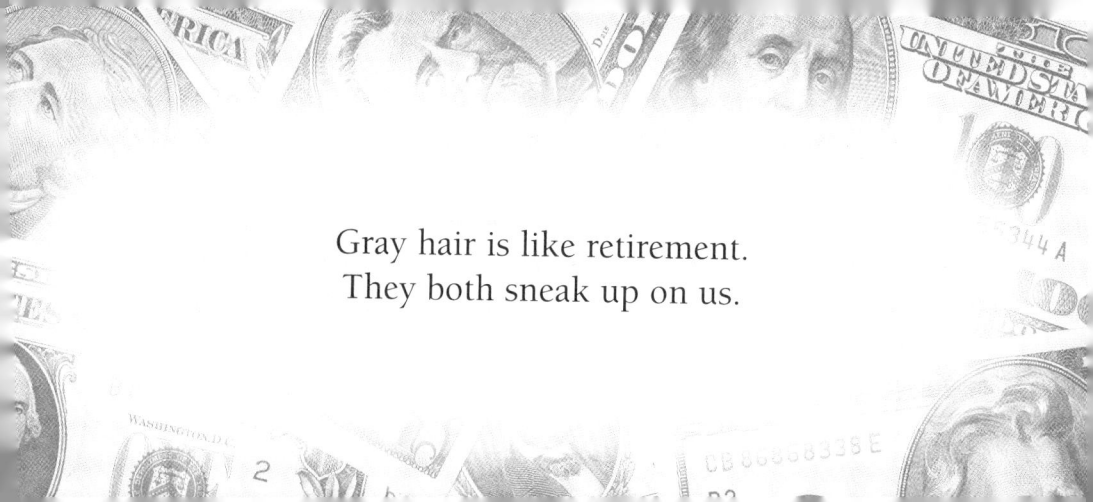

Gray hair is like retirement.
They both sneak up on us.

The same people that hate the rich
buy lottery tickets.

No one's credit is as good
as their money.

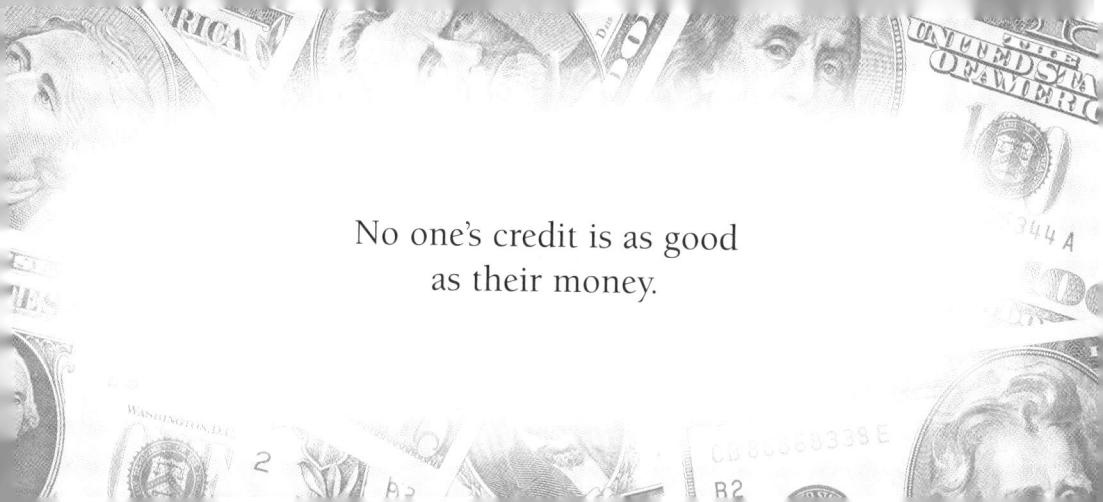

Investing is ninety-five percent research – the other half is luck.

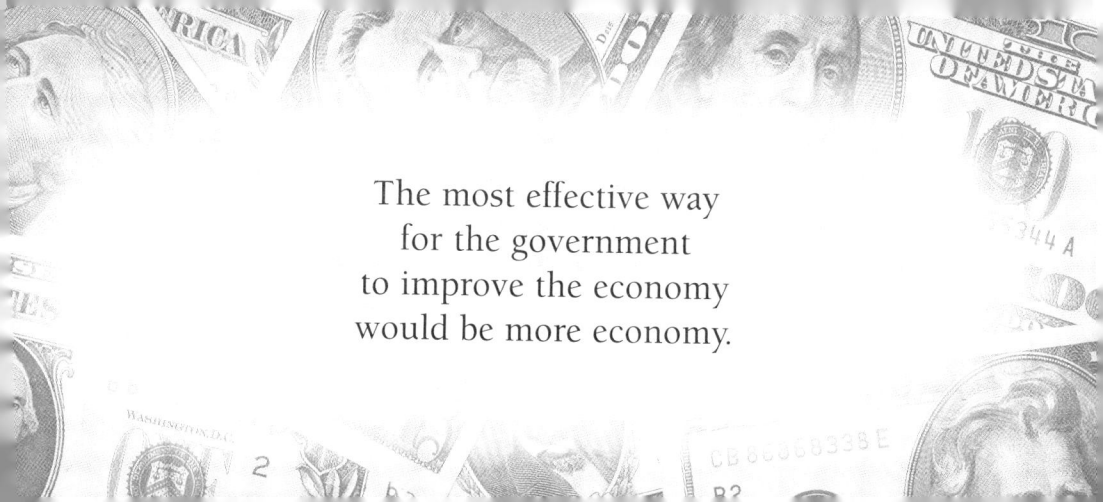

The most effective way
for the government
to improve the economy
would be more economy.

Money has a way
of making people interesting.

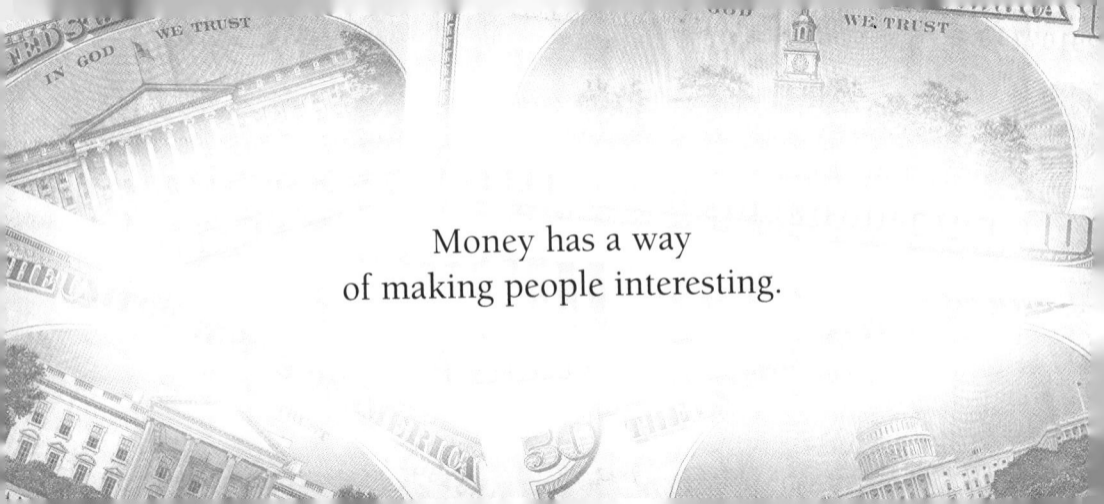

Money doesn't go as far as it used to,
but it sure goes a lot faster.

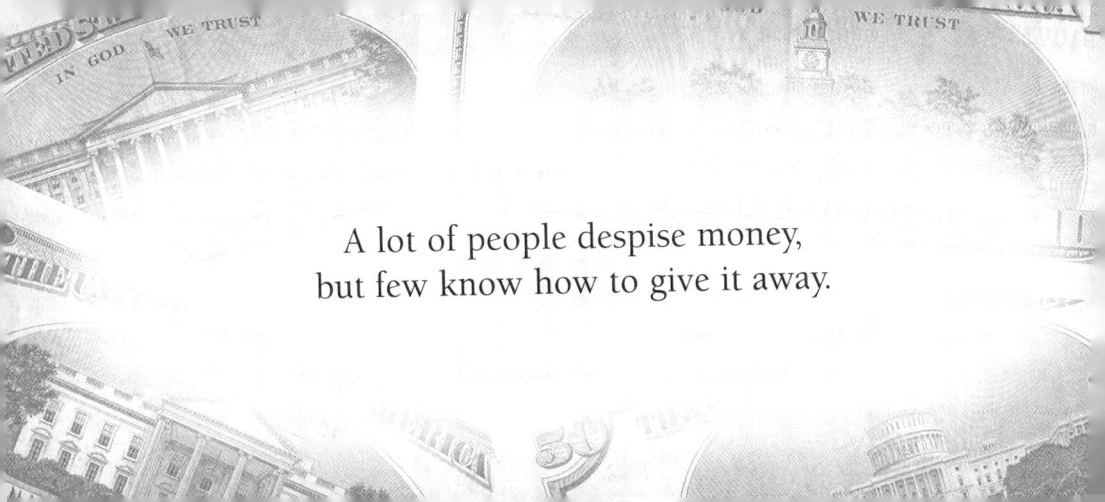

A lot of people despise money,
but few know how to give it away.

There was a time,
if something cost too much,
we didn't buy it.

Credit cards can buy one thing money can't – poverty.

If we avoid debt,
we won't have to avoid creditors.

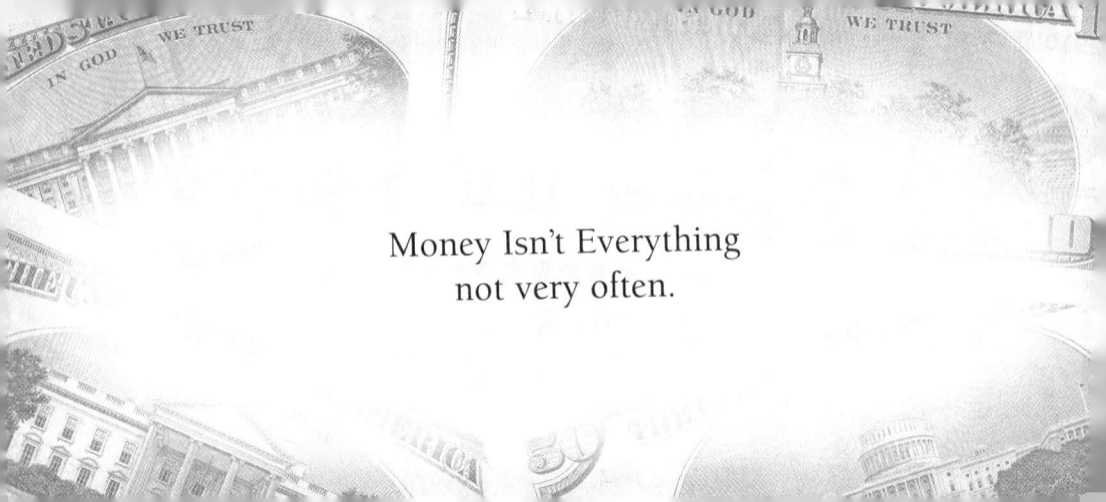

Money Isn't Everything
not very often.

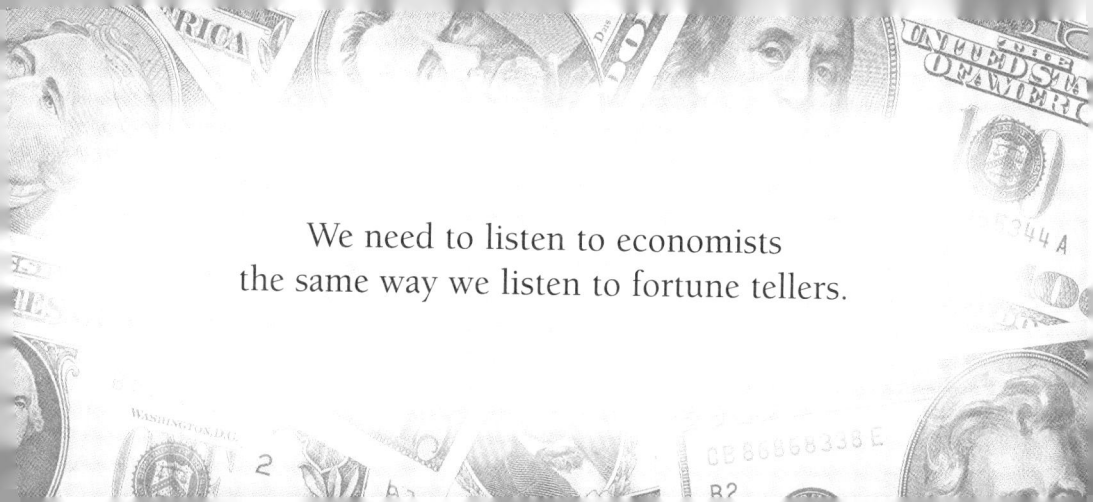

We need to listen to economists
the same way we listen to fortune tellers.

Money doesn't smell,
but not having any sure stinks!

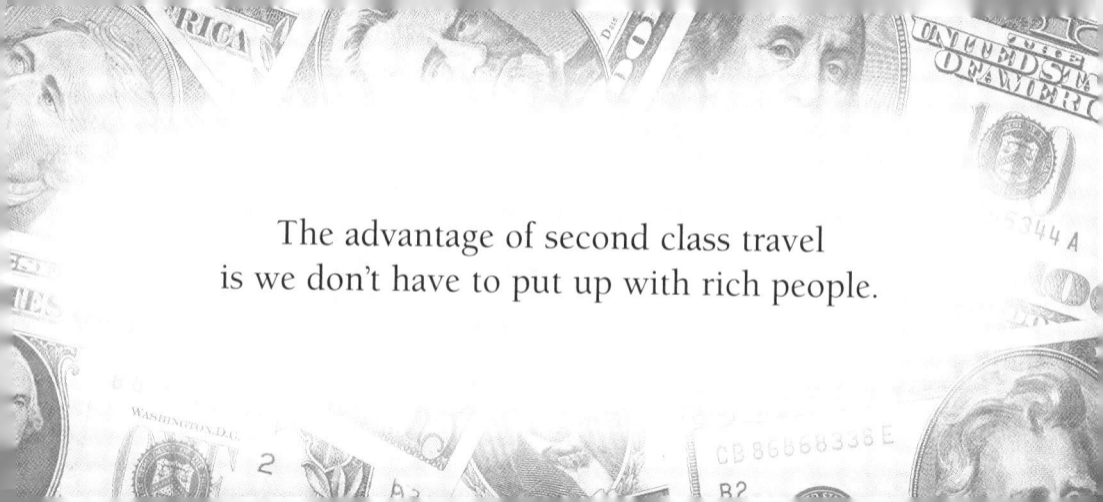

The advantage of second class travel
is we don't have to put up with rich people.

Easy Payments
are for things we don't need
and can't afford.

When the going gets tough,
the tough go shopping –
and when those shopping bills come in,
the going gets really tough.

They say a rich man can't be bribed,
but one can't help wonder
how they got rich in the first place.

Hush money can say a lot.

Money Isn't Everything,
yet people still treat others like nothing
if they don't have any.

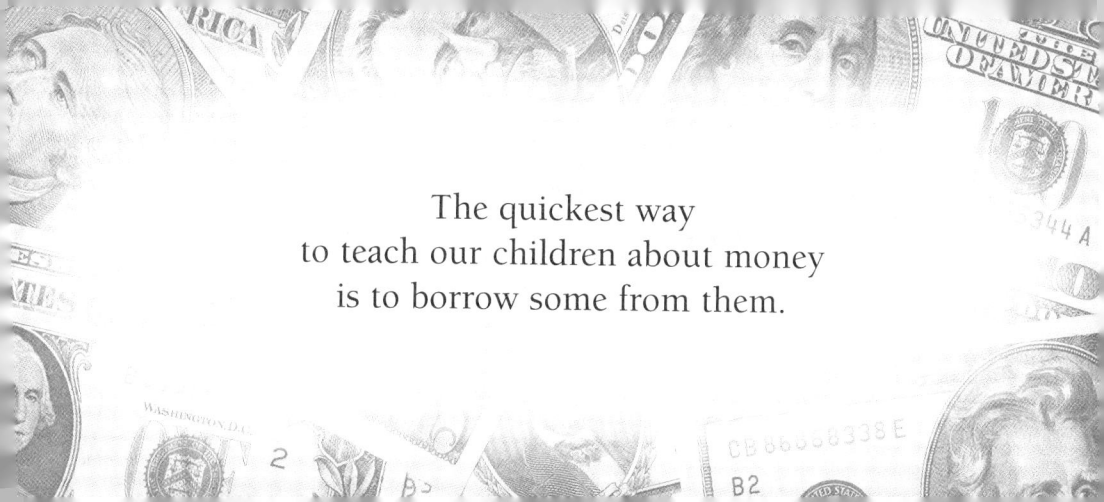

The quickest way
to teach our children about money
is to borrow some from them.

Cheap insurance can cost a lot of money.

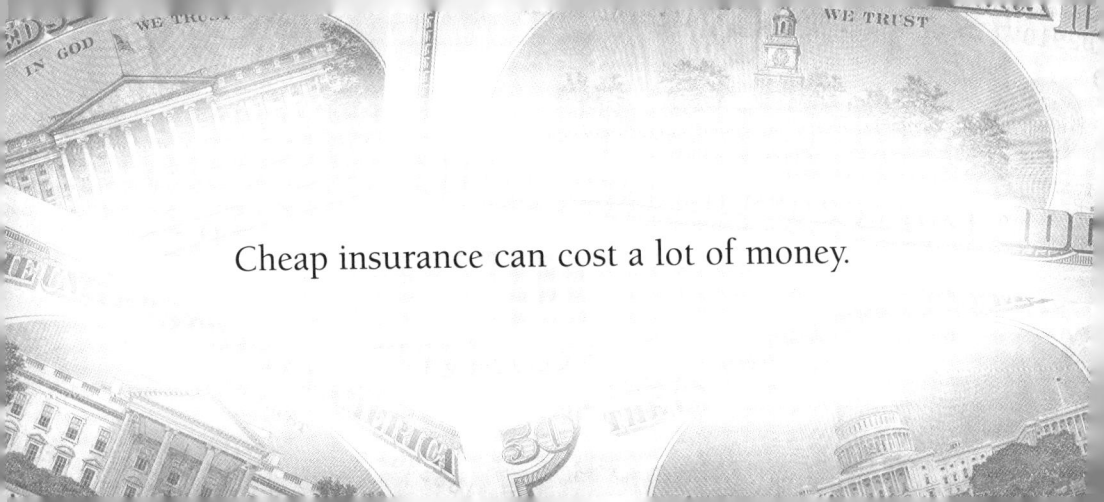

A person is rich if they can't count their money,
and poor if they are always counting their money.

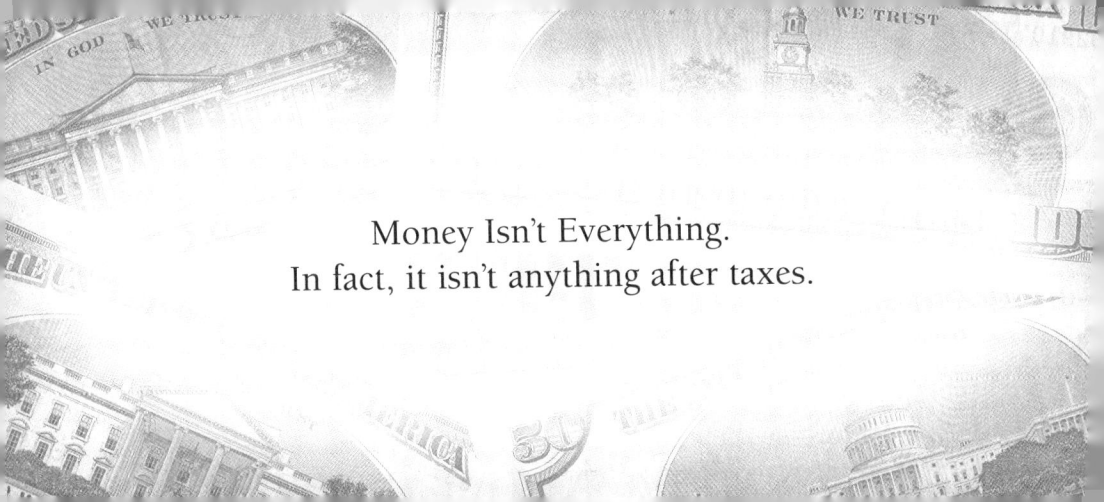

Money Isn't Everything.
In fact, it isn't anything after taxes.

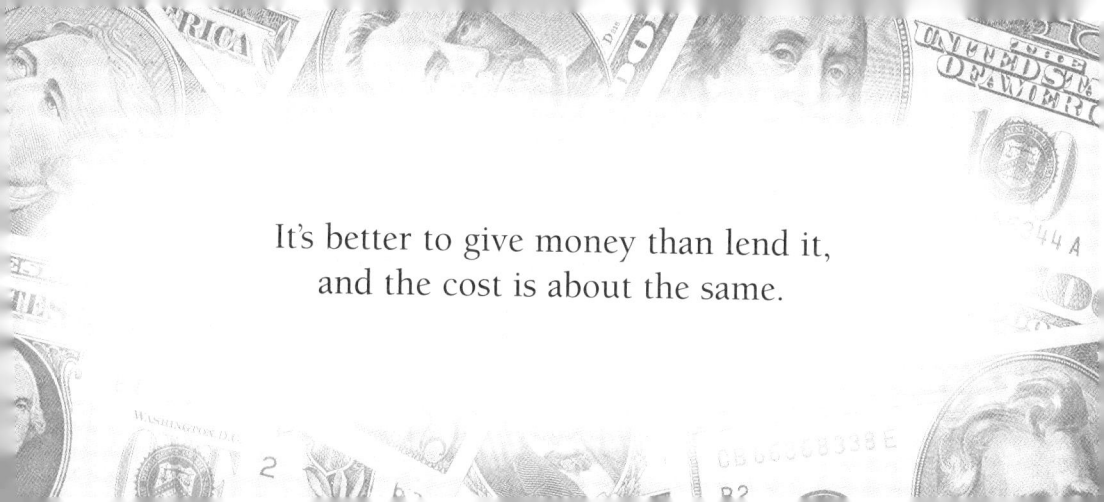

It's better to give money than lend it,
and the cost is about the same.

We all make a living by selling something.

If someone looks rich, talks rich, and acts rich –
it is a pretty safe bet they're not that rich.

Making someone a salaried employee
is a company's way of saying
they won't be paying them overtime.

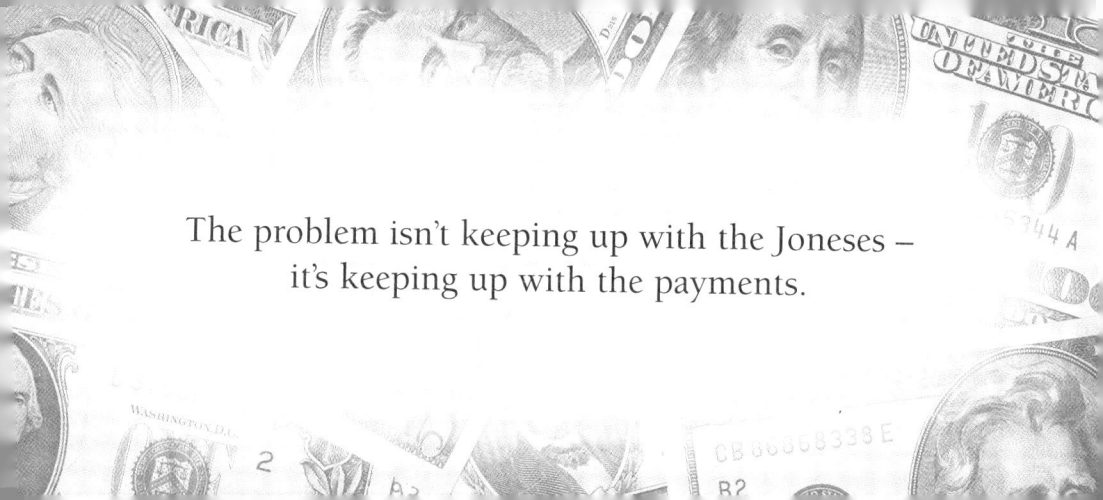

The problem isn't keeping up with the Joneses –
it's keeping up with the payments.

Remember, politicians aren't spending *their* money.

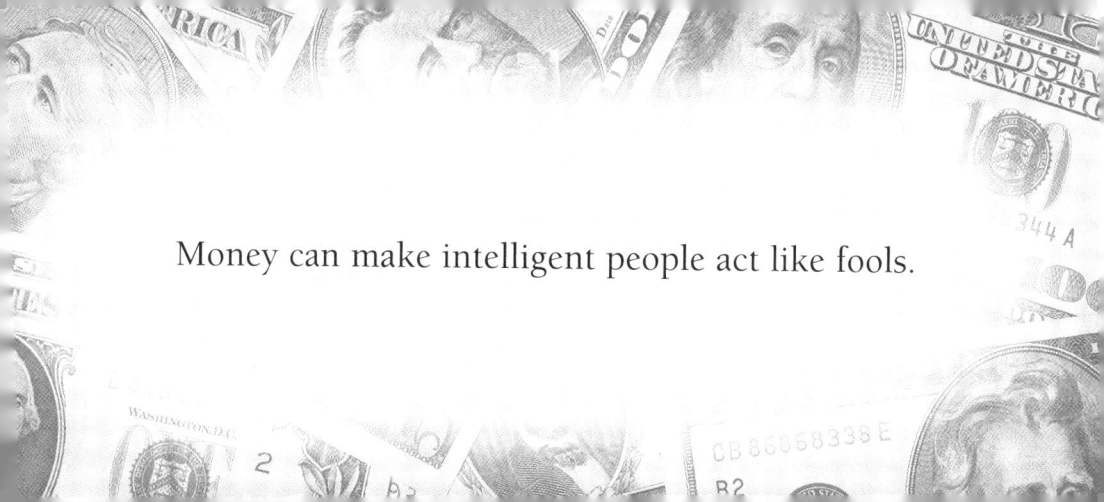

Money can make intelligent people act like fools.

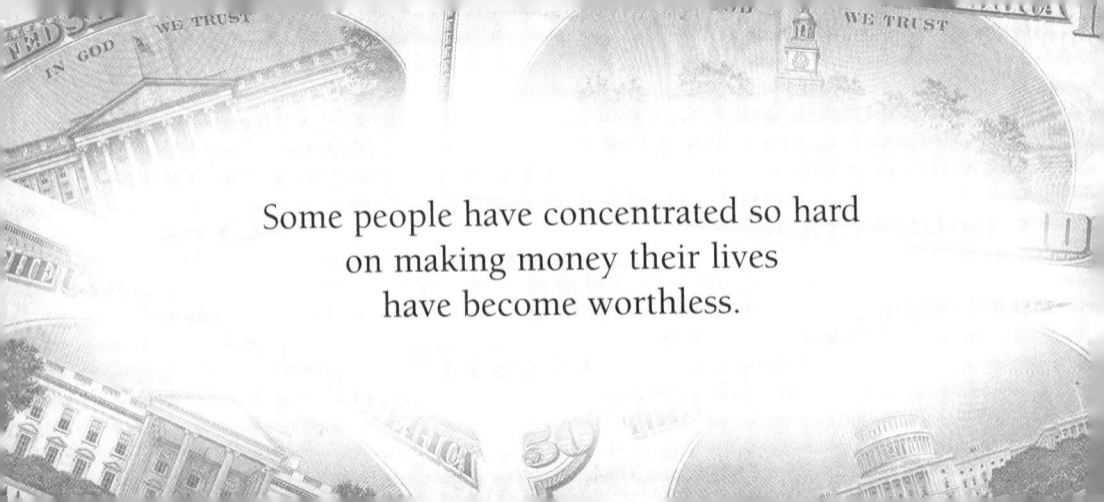

Some people have concentrated so hard
on making money their lives
have become worthless.

A car salesperson will tell us
a $30,000 sticker price is modest,
and a $700 rebate is substantial.

Less is More.
We get Less and it costs More.

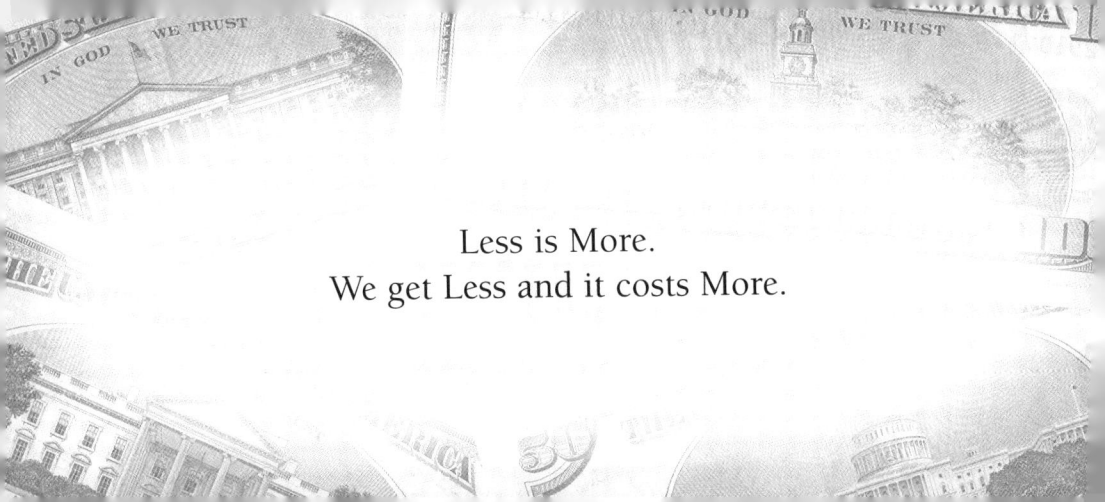

The rich are different from the rest of us.
They have more credit.

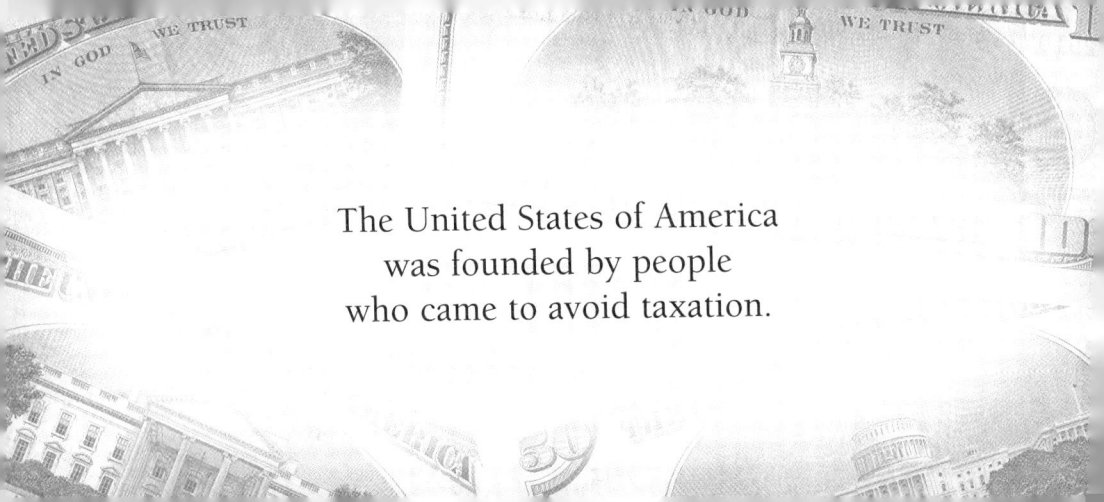

The United States of America
was founded by people
who came to avoid taxation.

Those who don't have enough money
to buy happiness – charge it.

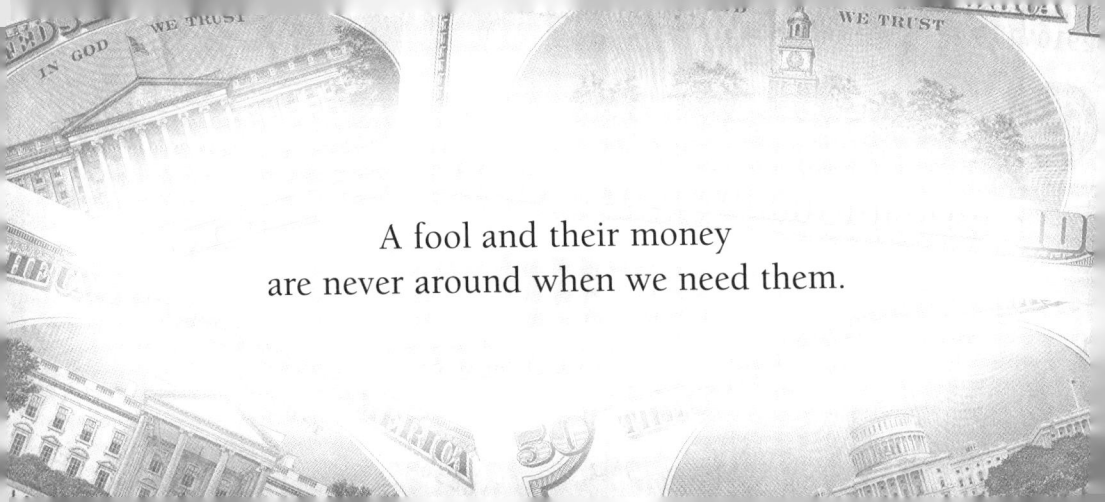

A fool and their money
are never around when we need them.

For most of us,
most of our money is spent
by the time we learn
to make the most of it.

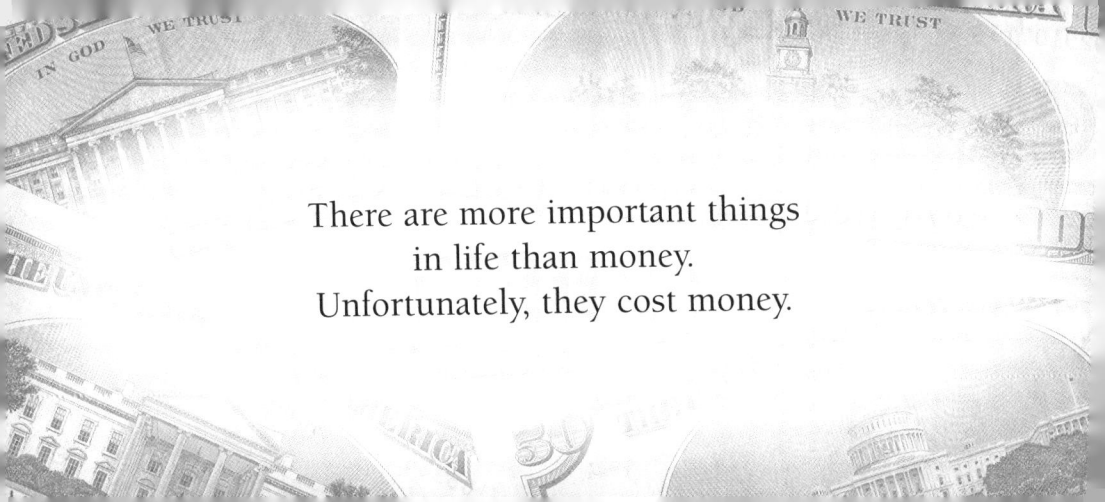

There are more important things
in life than money.
Unfortunately, they cost money.

There are few things
more troubling than having money –
not having money is one of them.

Don't expect to get wealthy
taking financial advice
from someone who isn't.

We all have money problems
whether we have money or not.

Ever wonder how the fool and their money got together before they were parted?

Money can't buy everything –
that's why we created credit cards.

ACKNOWLEDGEMENTS

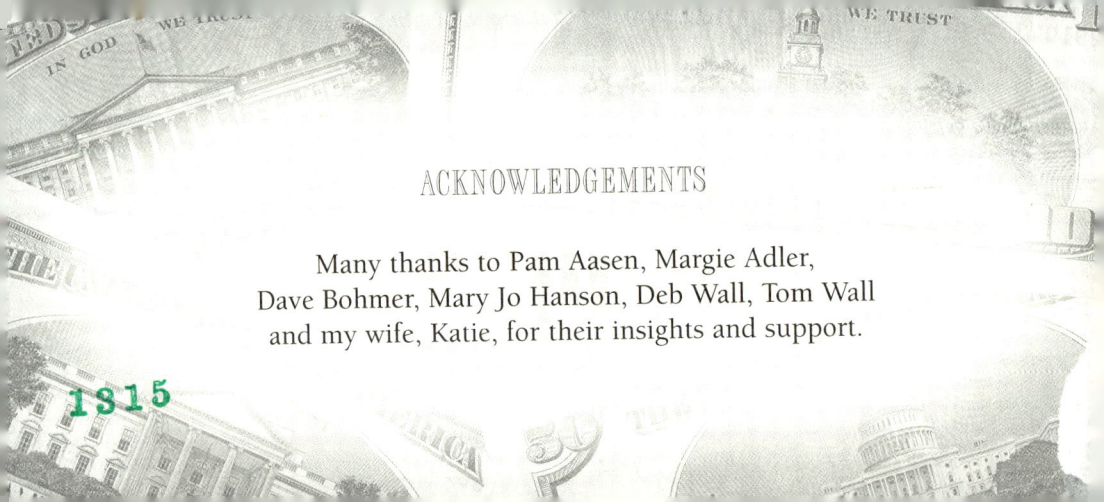

Many thanks to Pam Aasen, Margie Adler,
Dave Bohmer, Mary Jo Hanson, Deb Wall, Tom Wall
and my wife, Katie, for their insights and support.

NORMANDALE COMMUNITY COLLEGE
LIBRARY
9700 FRANCE AVENUE SOUTH
BLOOMINGTON, MN 55431-4399